The Teen's Guide to Understanding God's Design for Sex:

Christian Insights on Puberty, Sex Education, Dating, and Relationships for Teenagers.

BY

Michelle Dane-Smith

Michelle Dane-Smith

Copyright © 2024 Michelle Dane-Smith

All rights reserved. Unauthorized reproduction, storage in a retrieval system, or transmission in any form or by any means electronic, mechanical, photocopying, recording, scanning, or otherwise is strictly prohibited without the prior written permission of the publisher, as allowed under Section 107 or 108 of the 1976 United States Copyright Act.

Michelle Dane-Smith

TABLE OF CONTENTS

INTRODUCTION **11**

   Welcome to Your Journey: Understanding God's Design for Sex.. 14

   How to Use This Guide 19

CHAPTER ONE **23**

   Understanding Sexuality from a Christian Perspective.. 23

      Understanding Sexuality 24

      Sexuality and Relationships 25

      Emily's Confusion 25

      Scriptural Insights 26

      The Purpose and Beauty of Sex in God's Design 27

      Josh and Sarah 28

      The Beauty of Boundaries 29

The Bible and Sexual Morality: Key Scriptures Explained 30

Alex's Temptation 32

Embracing Your Identity in Christ 33

Mia's Journey 35

Living Out Your Identity in Christ 36

CHAPTER TWO 41

What is Puberty? Understanding the Changes 41

What Happens During Puberty? 43

Jamal's Growth Spurt 44

Male and Female Anatomy 45

Lily's First Period 47

Understanding Hormones and Emotions 47

Common Emotions During Puberty 48

Scriptural Insights on Emotions 49

Dealing with Body Image and Self-Esteem 50

Building a Healthy Body Image 50

Sarah's Struggle with Body Image 51

Boosting Your Self-Esteem 51

Jake's Journey to Confidence 52

Healthy Habits: Nutrition, Exercise, and Hygiene 53

Emma's Health Journey 55

Developing a routine can help you stay on track with healthy habits: 55

Navigating Puberty with Confidence 56

CHAPTER THREE 59

Friendship vs. Romantic Relationships 59

Understanding Relationships: 59

Friendship: God's Gift of Companionship 61

Romantic Relationships: A Special Connection .. 61

Jake and Emma's Friendship 62

Navigating Friendships and Romantic Feelings . 63

What is Love? Differentiating Between Lust, Infatuation, and True Love 63

Recognizing True Love 66

Setting Boundaries: Physical, Emotional, and Spiritual 67

Courtship vs. Dating: Understanding Different Approaches 70

Choosing the Right Approach for You 72

Navigating Breakups with Grace and Growth 72

Lucas's Breakup 73

CHAPTER FOUR 77

Digital Safety and Ethics 77

Understanding Digital Footprints 77

Rachel's Regretful Post 79

Why Your Digital Footprint Matter? 79

Biblical Guidance for Online Conduct 81

Social Media: The Good, The Bad, and The Ugly
.... 81

Emily's Struggle with Comparison 83

Navigating Social Media Wisely 84

Biblical Guidance on Social Media Use 84

Understanding and Avoiding Pornography 85

What is Pornography? 85

The Dangers of Pornography 85

Michael's Battle with Pornography 86

How to Avoid Pornography 87

Biblical Guidance on Purity 87

Online Predators and Staying Safe 88

Staying Safe Online 89

Sexting and Cyberbullying: Consequences and Prevention 90

Understanding Cyberbullying 92

Biblical Guidance on Handling Conflict 94

Navigating the Digital World with Faith and Wisdom 94

CHAPTER FIVE 97

The Power of Purity: Embracing Chastity 97

Understanding Purity and Chastity 97

Accountability Partners and Support Systems 100

Forgiveness and Redemption: Healing from Past Mistakes 103

The Role of Prayer and Scripture in Sexual Integrity 105

Incorporating Scripture into Your Life 107

Practicing Respect and Consent 107

How to Practice Consent 109

Biblical Guidance on Respect and Consent 109

Living Out God's Plan with Integrity 110

CHAPTER SIX **111**

Talking to Your Parents About Sex: Tips and Scripts 111

Starting the Conversation 111

Seeking Support from Your Church 113

Small Group Discussions: Learning Together .. 116

Trusted Adults and Who to Turn to for Guidance 118

CHAPTER SEVEN **123**

Role-playing Sex-Education Question and Answer 123

Q&A on Puberty 123

Q&A on Periods for Girls... 126

Q&A on Sex... 128

Q&A on Sexual Activeness Amongst Teens 131

Q&A on Same-sex Relationships and Homosexuality... 134

Q & A; How can I resist peer pressure to have sex? 137

Q & A; What should I do if I've already had sex and feel guilty? 138

Q & A; How do I talk to my boyfriend/girlfriend about setting boundaries? 139

Q & A; How can I deal with temptations and stay pure? 139

CHAPTER EIGHT 141

Journaling Prompts for Personal Reflection 141

Sam's Journaling Journey 141

Recommended Books and Online Resources .. 145

Apps for Accountability and Filtering Content 149

CONCLUSION 153

APPENDIX 161

Michelle Dane-Smith

INTRODUCTION

Sixteen-year-old Zoe slammed her bedroom door, tears of frustration and embarrassment stinging her eyes. She'd just had yet another excruciatingly awkward "talk" with her parents about...that topic. The one that made her want to melt into a puddle of cringe every time it came up.

Sex.

It wasn't that Zoe was naive or immature. She knew, in theory, about the **"birds and the bees"** and where babies came from. They'd covered the clinical basics in health class.

But the way her parents danced around the subject, flushing beet red and spewing lame euphemisms like "special hugs" and "God's secret wonderful," she couldn't help wondering if they viewed sex as something shameful. Taboo. An unfortunate biological necessity instead of the beautiful, sacred gift the youth pastor occasionally alluded to from the pulpit.

Zoe flopped onto her bed, exasperated. She loved her parents dearly, but they seemed to exist in a weird sexual paradox - acting flustered and awkward when discussing intimacy, while also embracing disappointingly antiquated ideas about gender roles and sexual purity.

Part of Zoe ached for someone - anyone - to give her the full, unabridged story about God's design for sexuality. No sugar-coating, no cringe-worthy euphemisms, no purity culture shaming. Just...truth. Unvarnished, liberating, life-giving truth about this core part of her identity and makeup.

As if on cue, her phone pinged with a new message from her small group leader, Amy. **"Don't forget, we're kicking off our new relationships/sexuality study this week! So, get ready for what's sure to be an awkward-FEST-load-of-fun"**

Zoe smirked at Amy's obvious sarcasm, but her heart still fluttered with a glimmer of hope. **Could this be it? Could this book - this promised journey into no-holds-barred Biblical wisdom about sex and relationships - be the answer to her prayers?**

Fueled by a swirling mix of curiosity, righteous indignation, and optimism, Zoe grabbed a notebook and pen, ready to immerse herself...

Michelle Dane-Smith

Welcome to Your Journey: Understanding God's Design for Sex

Hey there, beloved friends! If you've made it this far into the book, chances are you're intrigued, perhaps a bit nervous, and more than a little frustrated by the lack of honest dialogue surrounding sex from a Biblical perspective. No more shying away from the topic or Code Red awkward convos with the 'rents where everyone walks away more confused than when they started. This book is your official entry point into the unfiltered, understandable, undeniably liberating truth about God's design for sexuality.

Maybe, like Zoe, you've grown weary of the euphemism-laden talks, the eye-rolling clichés about waiting for marriage/guarding your heart, and the low-key shaming that can so often creep into teachings on sexual purity. You're starved for more - for wisdom, for candor, for insight that goes beyond the surface-level innuendo and equips you to understand and steward your sexuality with empowerment and integrity.

Or maybe you're on the other side of the "too much info" line, bombarded by a hyper-sexualized culture that treats intimacy as a cheap commodity. You've grown up in an era where pornography is just a click away, where hookup culture reigns supreme on high school and college campuses, and where dating apps have gamified the pursuit of romantic connection into a numbing cycle of swipe, smash, submit. The mixed messages and blatant exploitation have left you jaded, using your sexuality in ways that dishonor your body and heart.

Wherever you find yourself on this spectrum, we're so glad you're here. This book is an invitation to encuentro - to showing up for yourselves and each other with radical honesty as we explore God's design for the most mysterious, complicated, awe-inspiring aspect of our humanity. No sugar-coating, no shame, no dodging the tough stuff. Just truth that has the power to shatter lies and set you gloriously, profoundly free.

So, prepare to study the biblical text with fresh eyes, wrestle with modern realities of dating and relationships, get vulnerable about your own journeys and questions surrounding sexuality, and ultimately build a theology of intimacy rooted in the deepest wellsprings of sacred Scripture.

This book won't provide dry, clinical dissections of human anatomy or trite, one-size-fits-all formulas for "keeping yourself pure." Our exploration will be as multifaceted and robust as the topic itself, blending:

- ✓ Guidance for maintaining physical, emotional, and spiritual boundaries that honor God's design...while still embracing our identities as psycho-sexual beings.

- ✓ Unflinching looks at relevant cultural forces shaping how we view sex, consent, pornography, hook-up dynamics, gender identity, and more.

- ✓ Practical wisdom for navigating relationships (romantic and platonic), crushes, breakups, and discerning between lust, infatuation and covenant love.

- ✓ Studies of key biblical texts on intimacy, passion, sexuality, attraction, and God's original intent for the sacred "one flesh" union.

- ✓ Insights into pubescent changes (because when your voice cracks and pimples attack, you need all the help you can get!).

- ✓ Strategies for curating a healthy digital footprint, filtering toxic online content, and resisting the comparison traps social media can enable.

So, get ready, dear ones. This may just be the most candid, no-B.S. look at sexuality you've ever experienced. But we firmly believe that leaning into God's truth about the tremendous gift of intimacy will make you wiser, freer, and more empowered than you ever imagined.

Michelle Dane-Smith

How to Use This Guide

Since we're driving straight into one of life's most delightfully complex topics, this book is designed to be something of a road map - a candid, multidimensional exploration that covers all the bases, from the biological basics to modern cultural applications and everything in between.

At the same time, we want this to be a living, breathing conversation more than a dry, checklist-style study. Our hope is that by immersing yourself in the text, discussion prompts, personal stories, and biblical insights, you'll organically find your voice and begin formulating your own theology of intimacy aligned with God's heart and design.

With that in mind, we've formatted this resource as something of a choose-your-own-adventure experience. You'll encounter clearly sections and pathways for engaging whatever content is most relevant or pressing in this season. Want to start by simply understanding the pubescent changes your body is undergoing? We've got you covered. More interested in diving straight into the depths of theologically rich biblical texts on intimacy and sexuality? No problem! Looking for practical strategies and guidance around modern dating, hookup culture, navigating breakups, or curating a healthy digital footprint? It's all here!

Each chapter is designed as a self-contained study that can be read independently or in conversation with friends, mentors, families or small groups. You'll find:

- ✓ Engaging personal anecdotes that normalize/humanize the joys and struggles of stewarding sexuality well.
- ✓ Thought-provoking discussion questions to facilitate further reflection and dialogue.

- ✓ Scripture analysis & character studies focused on sex, passion, intimacy and romantic relationships.

- ✓ Practical tools and activity prompts for personal application (journaling exercises, role play scenarios, quizzes, discussion starters, etc.)

- ✓ Insights into relevant cultural topics like pornography, consent, dating in a digital age, and more.

- ✓ First-person stories from young people navigating sexuality and relationships with wisdom and integrity.

- ✓ And so much more!

Perhaps most importantly, since we're talking about such intensely personal, high-stakes subject matter, we want to create a safe space for you to show up authentically. To ask any and every question on your heart without fear of judgement or shame. To honestly work through the confusion, wrestle with temptation, and voice your doubts and insecurities. This is a guide, but it's one written with compassion, empathy, and the humility to acknowledge that none of us have this intimacy journey fully figured out.

With that in mind, please commit from the start to engage with this content responsibly and courageously. To push through the awkward surface-level barriers our culture has constructed around sexuality. And to bring your full, undistracted self to the study, reflection and discussion moments.

Let's get **STARTED!!**

Michelle Dane-Smith

CHAPTER ONE

Understanding Sexuality from a Christian Perspective

Caleb shifted uncomfortably in his seat as the youth group leader announced the topic for today's discussion: **sexuality.** He could feel his face flushing as a few snickers rippled through the room. Across from him, his friend Emily looked equally uneasy, fiddling with her hair and avoiding eye contact.

"I know this can be an awkward subject," the leader continued, **"but it's an important one that we need to understand from a biblical perspective. Who wants to start by sharing what comes to mind when you hear the word 'sexuality'?"**

An uncomfortable silence filled the room until a brave voice piped up from the back. **"Isn't it just about... you know... the physical stuff?"**

The leader nodded thoughtfully. "That's a common perception, but sexuality is so much more than that. It's a core part of our identity as human beings, created in the image of God. Let's dive deeper into what the Bible has to say about this amazing gift."

Understanding Sexuality

Sexuality isn't just about sex. It's about how we experience and express ourselves as male or female. It encompasses our thoughts, feelings, behaviors, and desires. In the Bible, sexuality is part of God's good creation. Genesis 1:27 tells us, **"So God created mankind in his own image, in the image of God he created them; male and female he created them."** This means that our sexuality is a fundamental aspect of our identity, reflecting God's image in us.

Sexuality and Relationships

God designed us to live in relationships with others. Our sexuality helps us form deep connections, not only romantically but also in friendships and family relationships. Think about your closest friends. There's a bond there that goes beyond just hanging out. You care about each other, share secrets, and support one another. This is a reflection of God's relational nature.

Emily's Confusion

Emily is a high school sophomore who loves her youth group. One day, she confides in her youth leader that she's been feeling confused about her feelings towards a boy in her class. She's not sure if she's ready for a relationship, but she feels drawn to him. Her youth leader reminds her that it's normal to have these feelings and that they are part of her developing sexuality.

Emily's youth leader opens the Bible to 1 Corinthians 13:4-7, which describes love as patient and kind, not envious or boastful. They talk about how real love is about more than just physical attraction; it's about caring for the other person's well-being. Emily feels reassured that her feelings are normal and that she doesn't have to rush into anything.

Scriptural Insights

The Bible gives us many insights into our sexuality and how we should live it out. In Songs of Solomon, we see a celebration of love and desire within the context of marriage. This book shows that sexual desire is a good and beautiful thing when expressed within the boundaries God has set.

In contrast, the Bible also warns against misusing our sexuality. In 1 Corinthians 6:18-20, Paul writes, **"Flee from sexual immorality... You are not your own; you were bought at a price. Therefore, honor God with**

your bodies." This passage reminds us that our bodies are temples of the Holy Spirit, and we should honor God with how we use them.

The Purpose and Beauty of Sex in God's Design

Now, let's dive into a topic that often makes people squirm: sex. But stick with me, because understanding God's purpose for sex can actually be pretty amazing.

From the very beginning, God had a beautiful plan for sex. In Genesis 2:24, it says, **"That is why a man leaves his father and mother and is united to his wife, and they become one flesh."** This verse highlights two important purposes for sex: unity and procreation.

Unity

Sex is a way for a husband and wife to become **"one flesh,"** building a deep, intimate connection that goes beyond just the physical. It's about emotional and spiritual unity as well. This bond reflects the closeness

God desires to have with us and helps strengthen the marital relationship.

Procreation

Another purpose of sex is to bring new life into the world. Genesis 1:28 says, **"Be fruitful and increase in number; fill the earth and subdue it."** Children are a blessing from God, and sex is the means by which new life is created.

Josh and Sarah

Josh and Sarah are a newly married couple in your church. They've shared with the youth group how they waited until marriage to have sex. They talk about the challenges and the blessings of waiting, and how it has strengthened their relationship. Josh mentions that it wasn't always easy, especially when they were surrounded by messages from the world that said otherwise. But they both felt it was important to honor God's design for sex.

Sarah reads from Hebrews 13:4, **"Marriage should be honored by all, and the marriage bed kept pure."** She explains how this verse guided their decision and how they now experience a deep sense of unity and joy in their marriage.

The Beauty of Boundaries

God's design for sex includes boundaries to protect us. It's like a fire: when contained in a fireplace, it provides warmth and comfort. But if that fire gets out of the fireplace, it can cause destruction. Similarly, sex within the boundaries of marriage is a beautiful gift, but outside of those boundaries, it can lead to heartache and brokenness.

The Bible and Sexual Morality: Key Scriptures Explained

Sexuality and morality are closely linked in the Bible. Let's look at some key scriptures that provide guidance on how to live out our sexuality in a way that honors God.

1 Corinthians 6:18-20

"Flee from sexual immorality. All other sins a person commits are outside the body, but whoever sins sexually, sins against their own body. Do you not know that your bodies are temples of the Holy Spirit, who is in you, whom you have received from God? You are not your own; you were bought at a price. Therefore, honor God with your bodies."

This passage emphasizes the importance of sexual purity. Our bodies are temples of the Holy Spirit, and we should honor God with how we use them. Sexual immorality isn't just a physical act; it affects our whole being.

Ephesians 5:3

"But among you there must not be even a hint of sexual immorality, or of any kind of impurity, or of greed, because these are improper for God's holy people."

Paul calls us to a high standard of purity. Not even a hint of sexual immorality should be present in our lives. This means being mindful of what we watch, listen to, and think about, and avoiding situations that could lead to temptation.

1 Thessalonians 4:3-5

"It is God's will that you should be sanctified: that you should avoid sexual immorality; that each of you should learn to control your own body in a way

that is holy and honorable, not in passionate lust like the pagans, who do not know God."

God's will for us is to be sanctified, which means being set apart for His purposes. Part of this involves controlling our bodies and avoiding sexual immorality. This requires self-discipline and reliance on God's strength.

Alex's Temptation

Alex is a junior in high school who has been dating his girlfriend, Rachel, for a few months. He really likes her, and they have a lot in common. But lately, Alex has been feeling pressured to take their relationship to the next level physically. He knows what the Bible says about sexual purity, but it's hard when he's alone with Rachel and things start to heat up.

One night, after youth group, Alex talks to his youth leader about his struggle. His youth leader shares 1

Corinthians 10:13, which says, **"No temptation has overtaken you except what is common to mankind. And God is faithful; he will not let you be tempted beyond what you can bear. But when you are tempted, he will also provide a way out so that you can endure it."**

They discuss practical ways Alex can avoid situations that might lead to temptation, like spending time with Rachel in public places or with a group of friends. Alex feels relieved to know that he's not alone in his struggle and that God will help him stay strong.

Embracing Your Identity in Christ

Understanding our sexuality is important, but it's also crucial to remember that our primary identity is found in Christ. Let's explore what it means to embrace our identity in Him.

i. **You Are Loved:** One of the most important truths to remember is that you are deeply loved by God. Romans 5:8 says, ***"But God demonstrates his own love for us in this: While we were still sinners, Christ died for us."*** No matter what mistakes you've made or how you feel about yourself, God's love for you is unconditional and unchanging.

ii. **You Are a New Creation:** When you accept Christ as your Savior, you become a new creation. 2 Corinthians 5:17 says, ***"Therefore, if anyone is in Christ, the new creation has come: The old has gone, the new is here!"*** This means that your past does not define you. You have a fresh start and the power to live a new life in Christ.

iii. **You Have a Purpose:** God has a unique purpose for each of us. Ephesians 2:10 says, ***"For we are God's handiwork, created in Christ Jesus to do good works, which God prepared in advance for us to do."*** Your identity in Christ includes discovering and fulfilling the purpose He has for your life.

Mia's Journey

Mia is a high school senior who has always felt like she didn't quite fit in. She struggled with low self-esteem and often compared herself to others. One night at a youth retreat, the speaker talked about our identity in Christ and how we are God's masterpiece. Mia felt something change in her heart.

she found encouragement in verses like Psalm 139:14, which says, **"I praise you because I am fearfully and wonderfully made; your works are wonderful, I know that full well."** Over time, Mia began to see herself as God sees her – valuable, loved, and with a purpose.

Living Out Your Identity in Christ

Understanding your identity in Christ is one thing, but living it out is another. Here are some practical ways to embrace and live out your identity:

1. **Stay Rooted in Scripture:** Regularly reading and meditating on God's Word helps remind you of who you are in Christ. Verses like Galatians 2:20, which says, "I have been crucified with Christ and I no longer live, but Christ lives in me," can help reinforce your identity.

2. **Prayer and Worship:** Spending time in prayer and worship strengthens your relationship with God. It's in these moments that you can hear God's voice affirming your identity and guiding your steps.

3. **Community:** Surround yourself with a community of believers who will encourage and support you in your walk with Christ. Hebrews 10:24-25 reminds us to "consider how we may spur one another on toward love and good deeds, not giving up meeting together, as some are in the habit of doing, but encouraging one another."

4. **Service:** Using your gifts and talents to serve others is a powerful way to live out your identity in Christ. Ephesians 4:12 talks about equipping God's people for works of service so that the body of Christ may be built up.

Jake's Transformation

Jake used to find his identity in sports. He was the star athlete at his school, but a knee injury ended his season prematurely. He felt lost and struggled with a sense of purpose. During this tough time, his youth pastor encouraged him to find his identity in Christ instead of his athletic achievements.

Jake started attending a small group and found new friends who accepted him for who he was, not just for his athletic abilities. He also began volunteering at a local food bank, discovering a passion for helping others. Through these experiences, Jake realized that his true worth came from being a child of God, not from his performance on the field.

Final Thoughts

Understanding and embracing your sexuality from a Christian perspective is about more than just knowing the do's and don'ts. It's about recognizing that your sexuality is a beautiful part of how God created you and that it should be expressed in ways that honor Him. It's also about finding your primary identity in Christ, knowing that you are loved, valued, and have a purpose in His plan.

As you navigate your teenage years, remember that you are not alone. God is with you every step of the way, guiding you and giving you the strength to live according to His design. Keep seeking Him, stay grounded in His Word, and surround yourself with a supportive community. You are wonderfully made, and God has an amazing plan for your life.

Michelle Dane-Smith

CHAPTER TWO

What is Puberty? Understanding the Changes

Mia stared at her reflection in the mirror, frowning at the sudden appearance of a few pimples on her forehead. "Ugh, why is this happening to me?" she groaned.

Her older brother, Zach, who was lounging on her bed, looked up from his phone. "What's wrong?" he asked.

"This!" Mia exclaimed, pointing at her face. **"I woke up with all these weird zits, and I feel like I'm getting taller by the day. Everything's changing, and I don't know what's going on with my body."**

Zach chuckled sympathetically. **"Welcome to the wonderful world of puberty, sis. We're all going through it, and trust me, it's just as confusing for guys as it is for girls."**

Mia sighed heavily. "I hate this. Why can't things just stay the same?"

Zach put his arm around her reassuringly. "I know it feels like your body is betraying you right now, but these changes are all part of God's amazing design.

Puberty can feel like a whirlwind. One day you're cruising through life, and the next, everything starts changing. Puberty is a normal part of growing up, and it's something everyone goes through. It's a time of significant physical, emotional, and psychological changes as your body transitions from childhood to adulthood. This chapter will break down what to expect and how to navigate these changes.

What Happens During Puberty?

During puberty, your body starts producing hormones that trigger a variety of changes. For boys, these changes usually begin between the ages of **9** and **14**, while for girls, it typically starts between the ages of **8** and **13**. Here's a basic rundown of what you can expect:

i. **Growth Spurts:** You'll experience rapid growth in height and weight. This can sometimes feel awkward, especially if your friends are growing at different rates.

ii. **Body Hair:** You'll notice more hair growing under your arms, on your legs, and in the pubic area. Boys will also start growing facial hair.

iii. **Skin Changes:** Your skin may become oilier, and you might start getting pimples or acne. This is normal and can be managed with good skincare habits.

iv. **Sweat and Body Odor:** Your sweat glands become more active, so you might start to notice body odor. Regular showering and using deodorant can help.

Jamal's Growth Spurt

Jamal was 13 when he suddenly shot up four inches over the summer. His clothes didn't fit, and he felt awkward and gangly. At first, he was self-conscious, but then he learned that almost everyone goes through growth spurts during puberty. His youth leader reminded him of Psalm 139:14, which says, "I praise you because I am fearfully and wonderfully made; your works are wonderful, I know that full well." Jamal realized that these changes were part of God's design for his body.

Male and Female Anatomy

As you go through puberty, it's important to understand how your body works. God created your body with incredible detail and purpose, and learning about it can help you appreciate it more.

Male Anatomy

For boys, puberty brings changes in the reproductive system. Here are some of the key parts:

- ✓ **Testes:** The testes (or testicles) produce sperm and testosterone, the hormone responsible for many male characteristics.

- ✓ **Penis:** The penis grows in size, and boys begin to experience erections and nocturnal emissions (wet dreams), which are normal parts of sexual development.

- ✓ **Scrotum:** The scrotum is the pouch of skin that holds the testes. It helps regulate the temperature of the testes, which is important for sperm production.

Female Anatomy

For girls, puberty involves changes in the reproductive system as well:

- ✓ **Ovaries:** The ovaries produce eggs and the hormones estrogen and progesterone, which regulate the menstrual cycle.

- ✓ **Uterus:** The uterus is where a fertilized egg can develop into a baby. Each month, the lining of the uterus thickens in preparation for a possible pregnancy, which is then shed during menstruation if pregnancy does not occur.

- ✓ **Vagina:** The vagina is the passage that connects the uterus to the outside of the body. It's also involved in menstruation and childbirth.

Lily's First Period

Lily was 12 when she got her first period. She felt scared and embarrassed, even though her mom had talked to her about it before. At youth group, the leader explained that menstruation is a normal part of becoming a woman and is actually a sign that her body is working the way God designed it to. They read 1 Corinthians 6:19-20 together, which says, **"Do you not know that your bodies are temples of the Holy Spirit, who is in you, whom you have received from God? You are not your own; you were bought at a price. Therefore, honor God with your bodies."** This helped Lily see her period as a natural part of God's design.

Understanding Hormones and Emotions

Hormones are chemicals in your body that regulate many different functions, including growth, metabolism, and reproduction. During puberty, your body starts producing higher levels of certain hormones, which can cause mood swings and strong emotions.

Common Emotions During Puberty

i. **Mood Swings:** One minute you might feel on top of the world, and the next, you're down in the dumps. This is normal and happens because of the hormonal changes in your body.

ii. **Crushes and Attraction:** You might start having strong feelings of attraction toward others. This is a natural part of growing up and learning about relationships.

iii. **Increased Sensitivity:** You might find yourself more sensitive to criticism or more easily embarrassed. This is also a normal part of emotional development.

Ben's Mood Swings

Ben was known for his upbeat personality, but during puberty, he started experiencing mood swings that left him feeling confused and frustrated. He'd be excited about a soccer game one moment and then feel inexplicably sad the next. At youth group, his leader shared Galatians 5:22-23, which talks about the fruit of the Spirit, including self-control. Ben learned that while his emotions were normal, he could pray for help in managing them and seek the Holy Spirit's guidance.

Scriptural Insights on Emotions

The Bible offers wisdom on handling emotions. In Proverbs 4:23, it says, **"Above all else, guard your heart, for everything you do flows from it."** This means being mindful of your thoughts and feelings and bringing them to God. Philippians 4:6-7 encourages us to bring our anxieties to God in prayer, promising that His peace will guard our hearts and minds.

Dealing with Body Image and Self-Esteem

Body image refers to how you see and feel about your body. During puberty, as your body goes through many changes, it's common to struggle with body image and self-esteem. Society often promotes unrealistic standards of beauty, but God's view of you is what truly matters.

Building a Healthy Body Image

i. **Celebrate Your Uniqueness:** Psalm 139:14 reminds us that we are fearfully and wonderfully made. Each person is unique, and that's something to celebrate!

ii. **Focus on Health, Not Appearance:** Instead of obsessing over how you look, focus on being healthy and taking care of your body as a temple of the Holy Spirit (1 Corinthians 6:19-20).

iii. **Positive Self-Talk:** Replace negative thoughts with positive affirmations. Speak truth over yourself, reminding yourself of your worth in Christ.

Sarah's Struggle with Body Image

Sarah always felt self-conscious about her height. She was taller than most of her friends, and it made her feel awkward. At youth group, they discussed 1 Samuel 16:7, which says, **"The Lord does not look at the things people look at. People look at the outward appearance, but the Lord looks at the heart."** This verse helped Sarah realize that her worth isn't based on her appearance but on her heart and character.

Boosting Your Self-Esteem

Self-esteem is about recognizing your value and worth. Here are some ways to build healthy self-esteem:

1. **Know Your Worth:** Remember that you are created in God's image (Genesis 1:27) and that He loves you unconditionally.

2. **Surround Yourself with Positivity:** Spend time with people who encourage and uplift you.

3. **Use Your Gifts:** Discover and develop the talents and abilities God has given you.

4. **Serve Others:** Helping others can shift your focus away from insecurities and remind you of your purpose.

Jake's Journey to Confidence

Jake was self-conscious about his acne. He avoided social events and felt embarrassed. His youth pastor shared 2 Corinthians 12:9, where Paul talks about God's power being made perfect in weakness. Jake began to see his struggles as opportunities for God's strength to shine through. He started volunteering at a local shelter, and serving others helped him feel more confident and less focused on his appearance.

Healthy Habits: Nutrition, Exercise, and Hygiene

Taking care of your body is an important part of honoring God's creation. Developing healthy habits during puberty can set the foundation for a lifetime of good health.

Nutrition:

   i. **Balanced Diet:** Eating a variety of foods from all food groups provides the nutrients your body needs to grow and function properly.

   ii. **Stay Hydrated:** Drinking plenty of water is essential for overall health.

   iii. **Limit Junk Food:** While it's okay to enjoy treats occasionally, try to avoid excessive consumption of sugary and processed foods.

Exercise:

i. **Stay Active:** Regular physical activity helps keep your body strong and healthy. Find activities you enjoy, whether it's sports, dancing, or hiking.

ii. **Exercise with Friends:** Working out with friends can make exercise more fun and motivating.

Hygiene:

i. **Regular Showering:** Keeping your body clean helps prevent odor and skin problems.

ii. **Oral Hygiene:** Brushing and flossing your teeth daily are important for dental health.

iii. **Skincare:** Washing your face regularly can help manage acne.

Emma's Health Journey

Emma used to skip breakfast and snack on chips throughout the day. She often felt sluggish and had trouble concentrating at school. During a youth group session on healthy living, the leader shared 1 Corinthians

10:31, which says, **"So whether you eat or drink or whatever you do, do it all for the glory of God."** Emma decided to make some changes, starting with eating a nutritious breakfast and bringing healthy snacks to school. She noticed a big difference in her energy levels and overall well-being.

Developing a routine can help you stay on track with healthy habits:

1. **Set Goals:** Make small, achievable goals for your nutrition, exercise, and hygiene habits.

2. **Plan Ahead:** Prepare meals and snacks in advance to make healthy eating easier.

3. **Stay Consistent:** Consistency is key to developing lasting habits. Find a routine that works for you and stick with it.

Matt's Fitness Plan:

Matt was always active in sports, but he didn't have a consistent exercise routine outside of practice. He decided to create a fitness plan that included running, strength training, and stretching. He also found a workout buddy to keep him accountable. They supported each other and shared Bible verses for motivation, like Philippians 4:13, "I can do all this through him who gives me strength." Matt felt stronger and more energetic, and he enjoyed the time spent with his friend.

Navigating Puberty with Confidence

Puberty is a time of incredible change and growth. Understanding these changes and learning how to navigate them with confidence is crucial. Remember that God has designed your body with care and purpose. Embrace the journey, knowing that you are fearfully and wonderfully made. Stay rooted in Scripture, maintain healthy habits, and seek support from trusted friends and mentors. As you grow and develop, keep your focus on honoring God with your body and your life.

By trusting in God and relying on His guidance, you can navigate the roller coaster of puberty with grace and confidence. Embrace this season as a time of preparation for the amazing plans God has for your future.

Michelle Dane-Smith

Michelle Dane-Smith

CHAPTER THREE

Friendship vs. Romantic Relationships

Understanding Relationships:

Chloe's heart fluttered as she spotted Jake across the cafeteria. As he laughed with his friends, she found herself mesmerized by his dimpled smile and the way his eyes crinkled at the corners.

"Earth to Chloe!" Her best friend Emma waved a hand in front of her face. **"You're doing it again - staring at Jake like he hung the moon."**

Chloe blushed furiously. **"I can't help it! He's just so...perfect."**

Emma rolled her eyes good-naturedly. "Uh huh, and how well do you actually know this 'perfect' guy? Besides his adorable dimples, of course."

As Chloe opened her mouth to protest, she realized Emma had a point. Her feelings for Jake went far beyond the bond of a typical friendship, but what did she really know about the depth of his character? About true, godly love?

Emma patted her arm reassuringly. **"Don't worry, girl. We've got you covered with a full relationship reboot - everything from friendship to dating to guarding our hearts. After all, this is about way more than just crushes. It's about honoring God's design for the most sacred bond of all."**

As you grow older, relationships start to take on new dimensions. You'll find yourself forming deeper friendships and possibly experiencing romantic attractions. Understanding the difference between friendship and romantic relationships is key to navigating this stage of life.

Friendship: God's Gift of Companionship

Friendship is one of the most beautiful gifts God has given us. True friends are there to support, encourage, and challenge us to grow. Proverbs 17:17 says, **"A friend loves at all times, and a brother is born for a time of adversity."** Friendships are built on mutual respect, trust, and a genuine interest in each other's well-being.

Romantic Relationships: A Special Connection

Romantic relationships involve a deeper emotional and physical attraction. These relationships can be wonderful but also come with more complexities. They require a greater level of commitment and understanding. The Bible talks about romantic love in Song of Solomon 8:7, **"Many waters cannot quench love; rivers cannot sweep it away."** This kind of love is powerful and requires careful handling.

Jake and Emma's Friendship

Jake and Emma had been friends since elementary school. They did everything together—homework, sports, and even family vacations. As they entered high school, they started noticing changes in their feelings. Jake began to see Emma as more than a friend, while Emma felt the same but was unsure about how to navigate these new emotions.

They decided to talk about it openly, realizing the importance of clear communication. They agreed to pray about their feelings and seek guidance from their youth pastor. This helped them maintain their strong friendship while exploring the possibility of a romantic relationship in a healthy, God-centered way.

Navigating Friendships and Romantic Feelings

1. **Open Communication:** Talk openly and honestly about your feelings with your friends.

2. **Prayer and Guidance:** Pray for wisdom and seek advice from trusted adults.

3. **Respect and Patience:** Respect each other's feelings and take things slow. There's no rush to move from friendship to romance.

What is Love? Differentiating Between Lust, Infatuation, and True Love

Love is a central theme in the Bible and is fundamental to our relationships. But not all forms of love are the same. It's important to differentiate between lust, infatuation, and true love.

Lust: A Physical Desire

Lust is a strong physical desire often based purely on looks or physical attraction. It's fleeting and self-centered. The Bible warns against lust in 1 Thessalonians 4:3-5, "It is God's will that you should be sanctified: that you should avoid sexual immorality; that each of you should learn to control your own body in a way that is holy and honorable, not in passionate lust like the pagans, who do not know God."

Infatuation: An Intense but Short-Lived Passion

Infatuation is an intense but short-lived passion or admiration for someone. It's often based on idealized perceptions and can fade quickly. While it can feel overwhelming, it's not a deep, enduring love. Proverbs 31:30 reminds us, "Charm is deceptive, and beauty is fleeting; but a woman who fears the Lord is to be praised."

True Love: A Deep, Selfless Commitment

True love is a deep, selfless commitment to another person. It's characterized by patience, kindness, and a willingness to put the other person's needs before your own. 1 Corinthians 13:4-7 beautifully describes this kind of love: "Love is patient, love is kind. It does not envy, it does not boast, it is not proud. It does not dishonor others, it is not self-seeking, it is not easily angered, it keeps no record of wrongs. Love does not delight in evil but rejoices with the truth. It always protects, always trusts, always hopes, always perseveres."

Mia's Journey to Understanding Love

Mia had a huge crush on a boy named Lucas. She was infatuated with his looks and charm. They started dating, but Mia soon realized that Lucas was more interested in physical attraction than a meaningful relationship. She felt used and hurt.

After talking to her youth leader, Mia decided to end the relationship and focus on understanding true love. She started praying for guidance and studying the Bible's teachings on love. Eventually, Mia met Ethan, a kind and patient boy who shared her faith. Their relationship was built on mutual respect, shared values, and a deep commitment to God and each other.

Recognizing True Love

1. **Patience and Kindness:** True love is patient and kind, always considering the other person's feelings.

2. **Selflessness:** True love is not self-seeking but puts the other person's needs first.

3. **Endurance:** True love perseveres through challenges and grows stronger over time.

Setting Boundaries: Physical, Emotional, and Spiritual

Boundaries are essential in any relationship. They protect you and help maintain healthy interactions. Setting boundaries in physical, emotional, and spiritual areas can prevent heartache and honor God's plan for relationships.

Physical Boundaries

Physical boundaries are about respecting each other's bodies and saving intimate acts for marriage. 1 Corinthians 6:18-20 advises, "Flee from sexual immorality. All other sins a person commits are outside the body, but whoever sins sexually, sins against their own body. Do you not know that your bodies are temples of the Holy Spirit, who is in you, whom you have received from God? You are not your own; you were bought at a price. Therefore, honor God with your bodies."

Emotional Boundaries

Emotional boundaries protect your heart and mind. Sharing too much too soon can lead to emotional entanglement and hurt. Proverbs 4:23 warns, "Above all else, guard your heart, for everything you do flows from it." Take time to build trust and deepen your emotional connection gradually.

Spiritual Boundaries

Spiritual boundaries involve keeping your relationship with God at the center. Encourage each other's faith, pray together, and study the Bible. 2 Corinthians 6:14 advises, "Do not be yoked together with unbelievers. For what do righteousness and wickedness have in common? Or what fellowship can light have with darkness?"

Noah and Grace's Boundaries

Noah and Grace started dating in high school. They decided early on to set clear boundaries to honor God in their relationship. They agreed to avoid physical intimacy, focus on building a strong emotional connection, and prioritize their individual relationships with God.

They had regular discussions about their boundaries and supported each other in staying true to them. Their relationship grew stronger as they respected each other's limits and encouraged each other's spiritual growth.

Tips for Setting Boundaries

1. **Communicate Clearly:** Discuss your boundaries openly and honestly with your partner.
2. **Seek Accountability:** Find a trusted friend or mentor to help you stay accountable.

3. **Pray for Strength:** Ask God for the strength to maintain your boundaries and honor Him in your relationship.

Courtship vs. Dating: Understanding Different Approaches

Courtship and dating are two different approaches to romantic relationships. Understanding the differences can help you decide which approach aligns best with your values and goals.

Dating: A Modern Approach

Dating is a modern approach to getting to know someone romantically. It often involves spending time together to see if there's a connection. While dating can be fun and exciting, it can also lead to pressure and confusion if not approached with clear intentions and boundaries.

Courtship: A Traditional Approach

Courtship is a more traditional approach that focuses on intentionality and commitment. It often involves families and mentors and is aimed at discerning marriage. Courtship emphasizes building a deep friendship and understanding each other's values and goals before making a commitment.

Alex and Sarah's Courtship

Alex and Sarah decided to pursue courtship instead of traditional dating. They involved their families and sought guidance from their church community. They focused on building a strong friendship and understanding each other's values and goals.

Throughout their courtship, they prayed together and sought God's guidance for their relationship. They felt a deep sense of peace and clarity as they moved toward engagement and eventually marriage.

Choosing the Right Approach for You

1. **Consider Your Values**: Reflect on your values and what you're looking for in a relationship.

2. **Seek Guidance**: Talk to your parents, mentors, and spiritual leaders for advice.

3. **Pray for Wisdom**: Ask God for wisdom and clarity in choosing the right approach for your relationships.

Navigating Breakups with Grace and Growth

Breakups can be one of the most challenging experiences, but they can also be opportunities for growth and self-discovery. Handling breakups with grace involves leaning on God, learning from the experience, and moving forward with hope.

Healing After a Breakup

1. **Lean on God:** Psalm 34:18 says, **"The Lord is close to the brokenhearted and saves those who are crushed in spirit."** Turn to God for comfort and strength during this time.

2. **Reflect and Learn:** Reflect on the relationship and what you've learned. This can help you grow and prepare for future relationships.

3. **Surround Yourself with Support:** Seek support from friends, family, and mentors who can provide encouragement and perspective.

Lucas's Breakup

Lucas had been dating Emily for two years when they decided to break up. He was heartbroken and struggled to

move on. His youth leader encouraged him to turn to God and read Psalm 147:3, **"He heals the brokenhearted and binds up their wounds."**

Lucas started journaling his thoughts and feelings, praying for healing and understanding. He also spent time with friends and focused on activities he enjoyed. Gradually, Lucas found peace and grew stronger in his faith. He learned valuable lessons about himself and what he wanted in a future relationship.

Moving Forward with Hope

1. **Trust God's Plan:** Believe that God has a plan for your life and relationships. Jeremiah 29:11 promises, **"For I know the plans I have for you,"** declares the Lord, "plans to prosper you and not to harm you, plans to give you hope and a future."

2. **Focus on Personal Growth: Use** this time to focus on your personal growth and relationship with God.

3. **Stay Positive:** Maintain a positive outlook and trust that God will bring the right person into your life at the right time.

Building Healthy, God-Centered Relationships

Navigating relationships and dating as a teenager can be challenging, but it's also an exciting journey of growth and discovery. By understanding the differences between friendship and romantic relationships, recognizing true love, setting healthy boundaries, choosing the right approach to relationships, and handling breakups with grace, you can build strong, God-centered relationships.

Remember that God is with you every step of the way. Seek His guidance, lean on His promises, and trust in His plan for your life. As you grow in your relationships, keep your focus on honoring God and loving others with the same selfless, unconditional love that He has shown you.

Michelle Dane-Smith

CHAPTER FOUR

Digital Safety and Ethics

Understanding Digital Footprints

Jared couldn't peel his eyes away from his phone screen, rapidly scrolling through an endless feed of memes, viral videos, and the highlight reels of his friends' seemingly perfect lives. A small part of him felt a twinge of insecurity as he watched their filtered snapshots of wild parties, romantic relationships, and spring break exploits.

His finger hovered over the upload button, ready to share his own carefully curated selfie that had taken him nearly a dozen tries to get just right. Maybe then he'd finally get those longed-for likes and validating comments.

Michelle Dane-Smith

"Hey man, what're you doing?" Jared's younger brother Lucas peered over his shoulder, catching a glimpse of the shirtless, ab-flexing pic. "Isn't that kinda...thirsty?"

Jared felt his cheeks redden as he quickly locked his phone. **"It's no big deal! Everyone posts stuff like this. You'll understand when you're older."**

Lucas just shrugged, leaving Jared alone with his device and his doubts. Was crafting an online persona really as harmless as it seemed? Or was there a darker side to this digital world he had yet to fully understand?

Every time you go online, you leave a digital footprint. This footprint is a record of everything you do on the internet—posts, comments, photos, and even the websites you visit. Think of it like footprints in the sand: they show where you've been and can sometimes be difficult to erase.

Rachel's Regretful Post

Rachel was excited to start high school and connect with new friends on social media. One day, she posted a photo from a party where she and her friends were being silly. She thought it was harmless fun, but later that year, she applied for a summer internship, and the organization found the photo. They questioned her judgment, and she didn't get the position.

Rachel learned the hard way that what you post online can have real-world consequences. She turned to Proverbs 12:18, which says, **"The words of the reckless pierce like swords, but the tongue of the wise brings healing."** This reminded her to be wise and thoughtful about what she shares online.

Why Your Digital Footprint Matter?

i. **Future Opportunities:** Colleges and employers often look at social media profiles. What you post can impact your chances of getting into a college or landing a job.

ii. **Personal Safety:** Sharing too much personal information can make you vulnerable to identity theft or online predators.

iii. **Reputation:** Your digital footprint affects how others see you. Posts can be misinterpreted, and negative content can damage your reputation.

Tips for Managing Your Digital Footprint

1. **Think Before You Post:** Ask yourself if what you're about to share is appropriate and if it could negatively affect you or others.

2. **Privacy Settings:** Use privacy settings to control who can see your posts and personal information.

3. **Delete Unwanted Content:** Regularly review your online presence and delete any content

that no longer represents who you are or could be harmful.

Biblical Guidance for Online Conduct

Ephesians 4:29 advises, **"Do not let any unwholesome talk come out of your mouths, but only what is helpful for building others up according to their needs, that it may benefit those who listen."** Apply this to your online interactions. Share content that uplifts and encourages others.

Social Media: The Good, The Bad, and The Ugly

The Good of Social Media

Social media can be a powerful tool for connection, education, and inspiration. It allows you to stay in touch with friends and family, learn new things, and share your interests with a broader audience.

John's Social Media Positivity

John loved using social media to share his passion for music. He posted videos of himself playing guitar and singing worship songs. His posts inspired others and even connected him with a local youth group band. John's positive use of social media brought him new friendships and opportunities to share his faith.

The Bad of Social Media

However, social media also has its downsides. It can be a source of comparison, leading to feelings of inadequacy and low self-esteem. Seeing others' highlight reels can make you feel like your life isn't as exciting or successful.

Emily's Struggle with Comparison

Emily followed several influencers on Instagram who seemed to have perfect lives. She started comparing herself to them and felt like she wasn't good enough. Her youth pastor shared 2 Corinthians 10:12, which says, **"We do not dare to classify or compare ourselves with some who commend themselves. When they measure themselves by themselves and compare themselves with themselves, they are not wise."** This helped Emily understand that everyone's journey is unique and valuable.

The Ugly of Social Media

Social media can also be a platform for negativity, including cyberbullying, misinformation, and harmful content. It's important to recognize these dangers and learn how to protect yourself.

Navigating Social Media Wisely

1. **Set Boundaries:** Limit your time on social media and take breaks if you start feeling overwhelmed.

2. **Follow Positive Accounts:** Choose to follow accounts that inspire and uplift you.

3. **Report and Block:** Don't engage with negative or harmful content. Report and block users who harass or bully others.

Biblical Guidance on Social Media Use

Philippians 4:8 advises, **"Finally, brothers and sisters, whatever is true, whatever is noble, whatever is right, whatever is pure, whatever is lovely, whatever is admirable—if anything is excellent or praiseworthy—think about such things."** Apply this to your social media use by focusing on positive and uplifting content.

Understanding and Avoiding Pornography

What is Pornography?

Pornography is any material (videos, images, or text) that depicts sexual content intended to cause sexual arousal. It's easily accessible online, but consuming it can have serious negative effects on your mind, body, and spirit.

The Dangers of Pornography

1. **Distorted View of Sex:** Pornography presents a false and unrealistic view of sex and relationships. It often objectifies people and reduces the beauty of God's design for sex to mere physical pleasure.

2. **Addiction:** Pornography can be highly addictive. It releases dopamine in the brain, similar to drugs, leading to a cycle of craving more intense content.

3. Relationship Damage: Consuming pornography can harm your current or future relationships by setting unrealistic expectations and reducing intimacy and trust.

Michael's Battle with Pornography

Michael stumbled upon pornography online at a young age and quickly became addicted. He felt ashamed and isolated, fearing judgment from others. Eventually, he confided in his youth leader, who shared 1 Corinthians 10:13, **"No temptation has overtaken you except what is common to mankind. And God is faithful; he will not let you be tempted beyond what you can bear. But when you are tempted, he will also provide a way out so that you can endure it."**

With the support of his leader and through prayer, Michael began his journey to overcome his addiction. He installed accountability software on his devices and joined a support group.

How to Avoid Pornography

1. **Guard Your Eyes:** Be mindful of what you watch and view online. Avoid sites and apps that may expose you to inappropriate content.

2. **Accountability:** Have someone you trust hold you accountable. This could be a parent, mentor, or friend.

3. **Seek Help:** If you're struggling with pornography, don't be afraid to seek help. Talk to a trusted adult or counselor.

Biblical Guidance on Purity

Matthew 5:28 says, **"But I tell you that anyone who looks at a woman lustfully has already committed adultery with her in his heart."** Strive to keep your thoughts and actions pure, honoring God with your body and mind.

Michelle Dane-Smith

Online Predators and Staying Safe

Understanding Online Predators

Online predators are individuals who use the internet to exploit or harm others, particularly young people. They often pose as peers or trustworthy adults to gain your trust and manipulate you.

Lisa's Close Call

Lisa enjoyed chatting with new friends online. One day, she started talking to someone who claimed to be a 16-year-old boy from another state. They quickly became close, but he started asking for personal information and inappropriate photos. Feeling uncomfortable, Lisa confided in her older brother, who helped her realize that the person was likely an online predator. They reported the account to the platform and blocked the user.

Warning Signs of Online Predators

1. **Too Much Interest:** If someone you meet online is overly interested in your personal life or wants to move the conversation to a private platform quickly, be cautious.

2. **Inappropriate Requests:** Asking for personal information, photos, or to meet in person are major red flags.

3. **Secrecy:** If they insist on keeping your relationship a secret or discourage you from talking about them to others, it's a warning sign.

Staying Safe Online

1. **Protect Personal Information:** Never share personal details like your address, phone number, or school online.

2. **Verify Identities:** Be cautious about who you interact with online. Verify their identity through mutual friends or other means.

3. **Report Suspicious Behavior:** If someone makes you uncomfortable or exhibits predatory behavior, report them to the platform and tell a trusted adult.

Sexting and Cyberbullying: Consequences and Prevention

Understanding Sexting

Sexting involves sending sexually explicit messages or photos via text or social media. While it might seem like a private way to express affection, it carries significant risks and consequences.

The Dangers of Sexting

   1. **Loss of Privacy:** Once an image is sent, you lose control over where it might end up. It could be shared without your consent, leading to embarrassment and reputational damage.

2. **Legal Consequences:** Sending or receiving explicit images of minors is illegal and can lead to serious legal consequences.

3. **Emotional Impact:** Sexting can lead to feelings of guilt, shame, and regret. It can also damage trust and intimacy in relationships.

Josh's Regret on Sexting

Josh thought sending a sext to his girlfriend would make their relationship stronger. However, when they broke up, she shared the image with others. Josh felt humiliated and isolated. He turned to Psalm 51:10, **"Create in me a pure heart, O God, and renew a steadfast spirit within me,"** seeking forgiveness and healing.

How to Prevent Sexting

1. **Understand the Risks:** Educate yourself about the dangers and consequences of sexting.

2. **Set Boundaries:** Agree with your partner on boundaries and respect each other's comfort levels.

3. **Seek Support:** If you feel pressured to sext, talk to a trusted adult or friend.

Understanding Cyberbullying

Cyberbullying involves using digital platforms to harass, threaten, or embarrass someone. It can be as harmful as physical bullying, leading to severe emotional distress.

Ava's Cyberbullying Experience

Ava was targeted by a group of girls at her school who spread rumors and posted mean comments about her online. She felt alone and hopeless. Her parents encouraged her to read Romans 12:21, **"Do not be overcome by evil, but overcome evil with good."** Ava reported the bullying, sought help from her school counselor, and found support from friends and family.

How to Prevent and Respond to Cyberbullying

1. **Be Kind Online:** Treat others with kindness and respect. Avoid participating in or encouraging bullying behavior.

2. **Report and Block:** Report cyberbullying to the platform and block the perpetrators.

3. **Seek Help:** Talk to a trusted adult, counselor, or mentor for support and guidance.

Biblical Guidance on Handling Conflict

Matthew 5:44 says, **"But I tell you, love your enemies and pray for those who persecute you."** Respond to bullying with grace and seek peaceful solutions.

Navigating the Digital World with Faith and Wisdom

The digital world offers incredible opportunities and significant challenges. By understanding the importance of your digital footprint, the impact of social media, the dangers of pornography, the threat of online predators, and the consequences of sexting and cyberbullying, you can navigate the online world with wisdom and integrity.

Remember, God calls us to live lives that reflect His love and truth. Colossians 3:17 reminds us**, "And whatever you do, whether in word or deed, do it all in the name of the Lord Jesus, giving thanks to God the**

Father through him." Apply this to your online presence, and strive to honor God in everything you do.

Michelle Dane-Smith

CHAPTER FIVE

The Power of Purity: Embracing Chastity

Understanding Purity and Chastity

Purity and chastity are about more than just abstaining from sex until marriage; they involve honoring God with your thoughts, words, and actions. It's about seeing yourself and others as valuable creations of God and treating everyone with respect and love.

Sarah's Commitment to Purity

Sarah, a 16-year-old high school student, decided to embrace a life of purity after attending a church retreat. She was inspired by the speaker who shared 1 Corinthians 6:19-20: **"Do you not know that your bodies are temples of the Holy Spirit, who is in you, whom you have received from God? You are not**

your own; you were bought at a price. Therefore, honor God with your bodies." This verse helped Sarah understand that her body was a gift from God and that she should honor Him with it.

The Benefits of Embracing Purity

1. **Healthy Relationships:** Embracing purity helps build relationships based on respect, trust, and genuine love, rather than physical attraction alone.

2. **Emotional Well-being:** Abstaining from premarital sex can protect you from emotional pain and regrets associated with premature physical intimacy.

3. **Spiritual Growth:** Living a life of purity strengthens your relationship with God and aligns your life with His will.

Practical Steps to Embrace Purity

1. **Set Clear Boundaries:** Determine and communicate your boundaries to your partner and friends. This helps prevent situations where you might be tempted to compromise your values.

2. **Stay Accountable:** Find an accountability partner who shares your commitment to purity and can support you in your journey.

3. **Stay Close to God:** Regularly read the Bible, pray, and attend church to stay connected to God and His guidance.

Biblical Guidance on Purity

Matthew 5:8 says, "**Blessed are the pure in heart, for they will see God.**" Strive to keep your heart pure by focusing on God's word and His plan for your life.

Michelle Dane-Smith

Accountability Partners and Support Systems

The Importance of Accountability

Having accountability partners and support systems is crucial in your journey toward purity and living out God's plan. These are trusted friends, mentors, or family members who encourage you, hold you accountable, and provide guidance when you face challenges.

Jason and Mark's Accountability Partnership

Jason and Mark, best friends since middle school, decided to become accountability partners. They both wanted to live out their faith and maintain purity. They met weekly to discuss their struggles, pray for each other, and study the Bible together. This support helped them stay strong in their commitment to God's plan.

Benefits of Accountability Partners

1. **Encouragement:** Having someone to encourage you and remind you of your goals can be incredibly motivating.

2. **Support:** When you face temptations or struggles, an accountability partner can provide the support and guidance you need.

3. **Honesty:** Knowing someone is holding you accountable can help you stay honest with yourself and others about your actions and intentions.

Choosing the Right Accountability Partner

1. **Shared Values:** Choose someone who shares your faith and commitment to purity.

2. **Trustworthiness:** Ensure your partner is someone you can trust with your struggles and who will keep your conversations confidential.

3. **Commitment:** Both of you should be committed to meeting regularly and supporting each other consistently.

Building a Support System

In addition to accountability partners, build a broader support system that includes mentors, family members, and friends who can provide wisdom, encouragement, and guidance.

Biblical Guidance on Accountability

Proverbs 27:17 says, **"As iron sharpens iron, so one person sharpens another."** Use your accountability relationships to sharpen each other's faith and commitment to living out God's plan.

Forgiveness and Redemption: Healing from Past Mistakes

Understanding Forgiveness and Redemption

Everyone makes mistakes, but God's grace offers us forgiveness and redemption. No matter what your past looks like, God's love is bigger, and He offers you a fresh start.

Emma's Journey to Forgiveness

Emma made some choices in her past that she deeply regretted. She struggled with feelings of guilt and shame until her youth pastor shared 1 John 1:9 with her: **"If we confess our sins, He is faithful and just and will forgive us our sins and purify us from all unrighteousness."** Emma learned that confessing her mistakes to God and seeking His forgiveness was the first step toward healing.

The Power of God's Forgiveness

1. **Cleansing:** God's forgiveness cleanses you from your past mistakes and gives you a clean slate.

2. **Healing:** Accepting God's forgiveness brings emotional and spiritual healing, freeing you from guilt and shame.

3. **Transformation:** Experiencing God's grace transforms your heart and helps you grow closer to Him.

Steps to Seek Forgiveness and Healing

1. **Confess Your Sins:** Honestly confess your mistakes to God and ask for His forgiveness.

2. **Accept God's Grace:** Believe that God's grace is sufficient and that He has forgiven you.

3. **Forgive Yourself:** Let go of guilt and shame, knowing that God has already forgiven you.

4. **Seek Reconciliation:** If your actions have hurt others, seek their forgiveness and strive to make amends.

Biblical Guidance on Forgiveness and Redemption

Psalm 103:12 says, **"As far as the east is from the west, so far has He removed our transgressions from us."** Trust in God's promise to completely forgive and redeem you from your past mistakes.

The Role of Prayer and Scripture in Sexual Integrity

The Importance of Prayer and Scripture

Prayer and scripture are powerful tools that help you maintain sexual integrity and live according to God's plan. They strengthen your relationship with God, provide guidance, and equip you to resist temptation.

Luke's Prayer Journey to Sexual Integrity

Luke struggled with temptation and felt overwhelmed by his desires. He decided to turn to prayer and scripture for strength. He started each day with prayer and read passages that encouraged purity. One verse that stood out to him was Psalm 119:9, **"How can a young person stay on the path of purity? By living according to your word."** This daily practice helped Luke stay focused on God and resist temptation.

The Power of Prayer

1. **Strength and Guidance:** Prayer connects you with God's strength and guidance, helping you make wise choices.

2. **Peace and Clarity:** Regular prayer brings peace and clarity, reducing anxiety and confusion.

3. **Accountability:** Praying with others can provide additional accountability and support.

Incorporating Scripture into Your Life

1. **Daily Reading:** Make it a habit to read the Bible daily. Focus on passages that encourage purity and integrity.

2. **Scripture Memorization:** Memorize key verses that you can recall in moments of temptation.

3. **Bible Study:** Join a Bible study group to deepen your understanding of God's word and receive support from others.

Practicing Respect and Consent

Understanding Respect and Consent

Respect and consent are fundamental to healthy relationships. Respect involves valuing others as God's creations, while consent means ensuring that all parties willingly agree to any physical or emotional interaction.

Megan and Tom's Relationship

Megan and Tom started dating and wanted to ensure their relationship honored God. They talked openly about boundaries and the importance of respect and consent. They agreed to 1 Corinthians 13:4-5 as their guiding principle: "Love is patient, love is kind. It does not envy, it does not boast, it is not proud. It does not dishonor others, it is not self-seeking, it is not easily angered, it keeps no record of wrongs."

The Importance of Respect

1. **Value:** Respecting others means recognizing their inherent value as creations of God.

2. **Trust:** Respect builds trust and strengthens relationships.

3. **Love:** Genuine love is rooted in respect and honors the other person's feelings and boundaries.

How to Practice Consent

1. **Clear Communication:** Always communicate clearly and ensure that both parties are comfortable with any physical or emotional interaction.

2. **Mutual Agreement:** Consent must be mutual and can be withdrawn at any time. Respect the other person's decision without pressure or guilt.

3. **Understanding Boundaries:** Recognize and respect each other's boundaries. Never assume consent; always ask and confirm.

Biblical Guidance on Respect and Consent

Romans 12:10 advises, **"Be devoted to one another in love. Honor one another above yourselves."** Apply this teaching by showing respect and seeking consent in all your interactions.

Living Out God's Plan with Integrity

Living out God's plan involves embracing purity, seeking forgiveness and redemption, relying on prayer and scripture, and practicing respect and consent. By following these principles, you can navigate relationships and sexuality in a way that honors God and aligns with His will for your life.

CHAPTER SIX

Talking to Your Parents About Sex: Tips and Scripts

Starting the Conversation

Talking to your parents about sex can feel awkward or uncomfortable, but it's an essential conversation to have. Your parents are likely your most trusted source of guidance and support, and they can provide valuable insight and wisdom.

Mia's Talk with Her Mom

Mia was nervous about talking to her mom about sex. She wasn't sure how to start the conversation or what her mom's reaction would be. Finally, she decided to sit down with her mom one evening after dinner. She began by expressing her feelings and asking if they could talk openly about sex. Her mom listened attentively and reassured Mia that she could ask any questions she had. Together, they had an open and honest conversation that brought them closer together.

Tips for Talking to Your Parents

1. **Choose the Right Time:** Find a quiet, private moment to talk when both you and your parents are relaxed and not rushed.

2. **Express Your Feelings:** Let your parents know why you want to have this conversation and how you're feeling about it.

3. **Be Honest:** Be honest and open about your questions, concerns, and experiences. Your parents will appreciate your honesty and vulnerability.

4. **Listen Actively:** Listen to what your parents have to say without interrupting. They may have valuable insights and advice to offer.

Scriptural Wisdom on Talking to Your Parents

Proverbs 1:8-9 says, **"Listen, my son, to your father's instruction and do not forsake your mother's teaching. They are a garland to grace your head and a chain to adorn your neck."** This verse emphasizes the importance of listening to your parents' wisdom and guidance.

Sample Conversation Starter:

"Mom/Dad, I've been thinking a lot about relationships and sex lately, and I was hoping we could have an open and honest conversation about it. I value your guidance and would love to hear your thoughts and advice."

Seeking Support from Your Church

Your church community can be a valuable source of support and guidance as you navigate questions and concerns about sex and relationships. Youth groups, mentors, and pastors can offer biblical perspectives and practical advice.

Alex Finds Support in His Youth Group

Alex felt overwhelmed by the pressures and questions surrounding sex and relationships. He decided to talk to his youth group leader, who listened compassionately and offered guidance rooted in biblical principles. Through his church community, Alex found support and encouragement to live according to God's plan.

Ways to Involve Your Church Community

1. **Join a Youth Group:** Participate in youth group activities and discussions focused on topics like relationships, purity, and biblical principles.

2. **Seek Mentorship:** Find a mentor within your church community who can offer guidance and

support as you navigate questions about sex and relationships.

3. **Talk to Your Pastor:** Schedule a meeting with your pastor to discuss any questions or concerns you have. They can offer biblical insights and prayer support.

Scriptural Wisdom on Joining a Church Community

Hebrews 10:24-25 encourages us to **"And let us consider how we may spur one another on toward love and good deeds, not giving up meeting together, as some are in the habit of doing, but encouraging one another—and all the more as you see the Day approaching."** Your church community provides a supportive environment where you can encourage and be encouraged by others.

Michelle Dane-Smith

Small Group Discussions: Learning Together

Benefits of Small Group Discussions

Small group discussions offer a safe and supportive environment where you can learn from others, share your experiences, and grow in your understanding of God's plan for sex and relationships. They provide opportunities for deeper conversations and meaningful connections.

Sarah's Small Group Experience

Sarah joined a small group at her church that focused on topics related to relationships and purity. Each week, they met to discuss a different aspect of God's design for sex and relationships, sharing their thoughts, questions, and struggles. Through these discussions, Sarah found encouragement and practical advice from others walking a similar journey.

How to Start or Join a Small Group

1. **Talk to Your Church Leaders**: Inquire about small groups available for your age group that focus on topics related to sex and relationships.

2. **Invite Friends:** Consider starting a small group with a few friends who share your interest in learning more about God's plan for sexuality.

3. **Be Open and Vulnerable**: Small group discussions thrive on openness and vulnerability. Share your thoughts and experiences authentically, and encourage others to do the same.

Scriptural Wisdom on Starting a Small Group

Proverbs 27:17 reminds us that "**As iron sharpens iron, so one person sharpens another.**" Small group discussions provide an opportunity for mutual encouragement and growth as you learn from and sharpen one another.

Trusted Adults and Who to Turn to for Guidance

Identifying Trusted Adults

Trusted adults play a crucial role in providing guidance, support, and mentorship as you navigate questions and challenges related to sex and relationships. They can offer wisdom, perspective, and practical advice rooted in their own experiences and faith.

Tyler Finds a Mentor

Tyler admired his youth pastor's wisdom and approachability. He reached out to him for guidance on questions he had about sex and relationships. His youth pastor listened attentively, shared personal experiences, and offered practical advice based on biblical principles. Through their mentorship relationship, Tyler found a trusted adult he could turn to for guidance and support.

Qualities of Trusted Adults

1. **Approachability:** Trusted adults are approachable and open to discussing sensitive topics in a non-judgmental manner.

2. **Wisdom:** They have wisdom and life experience that they can share to help you navigate challenges and make informed decisions.

3. **Faith:** Trusted adults have a strong faith foundation and can offer guidance rooted in biblical principles and values.

Where to Find Trusted Adults

1. **Church Leaders:** Pastors, youth pastors, and other church leaders are often available to provide guidance and support to young people.

2. **Teachers or Counselors:** School teachers or counselors can offer support and guidance in

navigating challenges related to sex and relationships.

3. **Family Members:** Parents, grandparents, or older siblings can serve as trusted adults who offer wisdom and support based on their own experiences.

Scriptural Wisdom on How to Find Trusted Adults

Proverbs 11:14 reminds us that **"Where there is no guidance, the people fall, but in an abundance of counselors there is safety."** Seek out trusted adults who can provide guidance and support as you navigate questions and challenges related to sex and relationships.

Seeking Guidance and Support

Navigating questions and challenges related to sex and relationships can feel overwhelming, but you don't have to do it alone. Your family, church community, small group, and trusted adults are all valuable resources that can offer guidance, support, and wisdom rooted in biblical principles. Remember, God has placed these people in your life to help you grow and flourish in your faith journey. Seek out their guidance and support as you seek to honor God in every area of your life.

Michelle Dane-Smith

Michelle Dane-Smith

CHAPTER SEVEN

Role-playing Sex-Education Question and Answer

Understanding and navigating through puberty, periods, sex, sexual activity, and same-sex relationships can be challenging and sometimes confusing. This chapter uses real-life scenarios and scriptural insights to answer common questions teens have on these topics. Let's dive into some role-playing scenarios to make these questions and answers more engaging and relatable.

Q&A on Puberty

Sarah and Michael Discussing Changes

Sarah and Michael are sitting at lunch, talking about the strange changes they've been experiencing. Sarah is 13, and Michael is 14. They're both a bit nervous and curious.

Sarah: Michael, have you noticed any weird changes in your body lately?

Michael: Oh, totally. My voice has been cracking, and I think I'm growing a mustache! It's so embarrassing. What about you?

Sarah: Yeah, my body is changing too. I've started developing breasts, and I'm not sure how to feel about it. Plus, my emotions are all over the place.

Q1: What exactly is puberty, and why do we go through it?

Answer:

Puberty is a time when your body transitions from childhood to adulthood. It involves physical, emotional, and hormonal changes that prepare your body for reproduction. For girls, it usually starts between ages 8 and 13, and for boys, between 9 and 14. These changes happen because your body starts producing more hormones like estrogen and testosterone.

Scriptural Insight on Puberty:

Psalm 139:14 says, **"I praise you because I am fearfully and wonderfully made; your works are wonderful, I know that full well."** Puberty is part of God's amazing design for your body, and even though it can be awkward, it's a natural and important process.

Q2: Why are my emotions so intense during puberty?

Answer:

During puberty, your body produces a lot of hormones that can affect your mood and emotions. This is completely normal. It can help to talk about your feelings with trusted friends, family members, or mentors, and remember that you're not alone.

Scriptural Insight on Mood Swing:

Philippians 4:6-7 encourages us, **"Do not be anxious about anything, but in every situation, by prayer and petition, with thanksgiving, present your requests to God. And the peace of God, which transcends all understanding, will guard your hearts and your minds in Christ Jesus."** God cares about your feelings and wants to give you peace.

Q&A on Periods for Girls

Emily's First Period

Emily is at home, feeling worried. She calls her older cousin, Anna, to talk about something unexpected.

Emily: Anna, I think I just got my first period, and I'm freaking out. What do I do?

Anna: Don't worry, Emily. It's completely normal and part of growing up. Let's talk about it.

Q1: What is a period, and why does it happen?

Answer:

A period, or menstruation, is when the lining of the uterus sheds through the vagina. It happens because the body is preparing for the possibility of pregnancy each month. If there's no pregnancy, the lining isn't needed, so it's shed. This cycle typically happens every 28-30 days but can vary.

Q2: How can I manage my period, and what products should I use?

Answer:

There are several products you can use to manage your period, including pads, tampons, and menstrual cups. It's important to choose what's most comfortable for you. Make sure to change your pads or tampons regularly to stay clean and avoid any infections. Additionally, keeping a period calendar can help you track your cycle and be prepared.

Q&A on Sex

Jake and Lauren Talking About Relationships

Jake and Lauren are best friends. They often talk about life and the future. Today, their conversation turns to a serious topic.

Jake: Lauren, I've been hearing a lot about sex at school, and it's confusing. Why is it such a big deal?

Lauren: Yeah, I know what you mean. Let's figure it out together.

Q1: What is the purpose of sex according to the Bible?

Answer:

Sex is a beautiful gift from God designed for marriage. It's meant to create a deep bond between a husband and wife and is also part of God's design for procreation. Within the context of marriage, sex is a way to express love, intimacy, and unity.

Scriptural Insight on Sex:

Genesis 2:24 says, **"That is why a man leaves his father and mother and is united to his wife, and they become one flesh."** This verse highlights the unity and special bond that sex creates within marriage.

Q2: Why should we wait until marriage to have sex?

Answer:

Waiting until marriage to have sex honors God's design and helps protect your emotional and spiritual well-being. Premarital sex can lead to emotional pain, broken relationships, and even physical consequences. By waiting, you are building a foundation of trust and commitment with your future spouse.

Scriptural Insight on Pre-marital Sex:

1 Thessalonians 4:3-4 instructs us, **"It is God's will that you should be sanctified: that you should avoid sexual immorality; that each of you should learn to control your own body in a way that is holy and honorable."** God's desire is for you to live a holy life, including in your sexual behavior.

Q&A on Sexual Activeness Amongst Teens

Peer Pressure at a Party

Ben is at a party where some of his friends are talking about their sexual experiences. He feels pressured and unsure of what to do. He steps outside and calls his older brother, Alex.

Ben: Alex, everyone at this party is talking about sex like it's no big deal. Am I missing out?

Alex: I understand how you feel, Ben. It's important to remember why you're making your choices. Let's talk about it.

Q1: Is it normal to feel pressure to be sexually active?

Answer:

Yes, it's normal to feel pressure, especially from peers and media. However, just because something is common doesn't mean it's right for you. It's important to make decisions based on your values and beliefs, not on pressure from others.

Scriptural Insight on Sexual Activeness:

Romans 12:2 advises, **"Do not conform to the pattern of this world, but be transformed by the renewing of your mind. Then you will be able to test and approve what God's will is—his good, pleasing and perfect will."** Stand firm in your faith and make choices that align with God's will.

Q2: How can I handle peer pressure about sex?

Answer:

Handling peer pressure can be tough, but it's important to stay true to your values. **Here are a few tips:**

- ✓ **Know Your Boundaries:** Clearly define your boundaries before you're in a pressured situation.

- ✓ **Have a Response Ready:** Practice what you'll say if someone pressures you.

- ✓ **Seek Support:** Surround yourself with friends who respect your choices.

- ✓ **Pray for Strength:** Ask God for the courage to stand firm in your beliefs.

Scriptural Insight on Peer Pressure:

1 Corinthians 10:13 reassures us, **"No temptation has overtaken you except what is common to mankind. And God is faithful; he will not let you be tempted beyond what you can bear. But when you are tempted, he will also provide a way out so that you can endure it."** God provides strength and a way out of every temptation.

Michelle Dane-Smith

Q&A on Same-sex Relationships and Homosexuality

Ashley and Her Same-sex Confusion

Ashley has been feeling confused about her feelings towards her best friend, another girl. She decides to talk to her youth group leader, Mrs. Johnson, about it.*

Ashley: Mrs. Johnson, I've been feeling things for my best friend that confuse me. I don't know what to do or how to think about it.

Mrs. Johnson: Thank you for sharing, Ashley. Let's talk through this together with love and understanding.

Q1: What does the Bible say about same-sex relationships?

Answer:

The Bible addresses same-sex relationships in several passages. It teaches that God's design for marriage and sexual relationships is between a man and a woman.

This design is rooted in creation and is intended for procreation and reflecting the union between Christ and the church.

Scriptural Insight:

Romans 1:26-27 and 1 Corinthians 6:9-10 discuss same-sex relationships. These passages can be challenging, but it's important to read them in the context of God's love and the overall message of redemption and transformation through Jesus Christ.

Q2: How should I handle my feelings and questions about same-sex attraction?

Answer:

It's important to approach your feelings and questions with honesty and seek guidance in a safe, loving environment. Here are some steps:

- ✓ **Pray for Guidance:** Ask God for wisdom and clarity about your feelings.

- ✓ **Seek Support:** Talk to trusted adults, mentors, or counselors who can provide biblical guidance and support.

- ✓ **Study Scripture:** Spend time studying what the Bible says about sexuality and relationships.

- ✓ **Find Community:** Join a church or support group where you can discuss your feelings in a safe and non-judgmental space.

Scriptural Insight:

Galatians 6:2 encourages us to **"Carry each other's burdens, and in this way you will fulfill the law of Christ."** It's important to support one another with love and understanding.

Q & A on Why is waiting until marriage to have sex important?

Answer

Waiting until marriage to have sex is important because it aligns with God's design for sexuality. Hebrews 13:4 says, **"Marriage should be honored by all, and the marriage bed kept pure, for God will judge the adulterer and all the sexually immoral."** Sex is a beautiful gift from God meant to be enjoyed within the commitment and safety of marriage. It helps build a strong, trusting foundation for your relationship.

Q & A; How can I resist peer pressure to have sex?

Answer:

Resisting peer pressure can be challenging, but remember that your worth comes from God, not from what others think. Romans 12:2 encourages us, **"Do not conform to the pattern of this world, but be**

transformed by the renewing of your mind." Surround yourself with friends who share your values, set clear boundaries, and stay connected to God through prayer and scripture.

Q & A; What should I do if I've already had sex and feel guilty?

Answer:

If you've already had sex and feel guilty, know that God's grace is greater than any mistake. 1 John 1:9 reassures us, **"If we confess our sins, He is faithful and just and will forgive us our sins and purify us from all unrighteousness."** Seek God's forgiveness, talk to a trusted adult or mentor, and commit to living according to His plan from now on.

Michelle Dane-Smith

Q & A; How do I talk to my boyfriend/girlfriend about setting boundaries?

Answer:

Communicate openly and honestly with your boyfriend/girlfriend about your commitment to purity. Use "I" statements to express your feelings and beliefs. For example, **"I believe in waiting until marriage to have sex because I want to honor God and build a strong foundation for our relationship."** Set clear boundaries together and hold each other accountable.

Q & A; How can I deal with temptations and stay pure?

Answer

Dealing with temptations requires vigilance and support. 1 Corinthians 10:13 offers hope: **"No temptation has overtaken you except what is common to mankind. And God is faithful; He will**

not let you be tempted beyond what you can bear. But when you are tempted, He will also provide a way out so that you can endure it." Pray for strength, avoid situations that may lead to temptation, and stay accountable to a trusted friend or mentor.

Final Thoughts

Navigating puberty, periods, sex, sexual activity, and same-sex relationships can be challenging, but you don't have to do it alone. God is with you every step of the way, and He has placed people in your life to support and guide you. Always seek His wisdom through prayer and Scripture, and lean on your community for support. Remember, you are fearfully and wonderfully made, and God has an amazing plan for your life.

Michelle Dane-Smith

CHAPTER EIGHT

Journaling Prompts for Personal Reflection

Journaling is a powerful tool for personal growth and reflection. It helps you process your thoughts, emotions, and experiences while deepening your relationship with God. By putting your feelings into words, you can gain clarity and insight into your journey toward understanding God's design for sexuality.

Sam's Journaling Journey

Sam, a 15-year-old high school sophomore, started journaling after his youth pastor suggested it. At first, he wasn't sure what to write about, but over time, he found that journaling helped him sort through his feelings and understand his faith better. Sam found particular comfort in reflecting on scriptures and writing about his struggles and victories.

Benefits of Journaling

1. **Self-Discovery:** Helps you understand yourself better.

2. **Spiritual Growth:** Deepens your relationship with God.

3. **Emotional Healing:** Provides an outlet for expressing and processing emotions.

4. **Personal Accountability:** Keeps track of your progress and setbacks.

Journaling Prompts

1. **Reflection on Scripture:**

   - "Read 1 Corinthians 6:19-20. How does this verse shape your view of your body and sexuality?"

- "Reflect on Psalm 139:14. Write about what it means to be 'fearfully and wonderfully made'."

2. **Personal Struggles and Victories:**

- "Write about a recent struggle you faced regarding purity. How did you handle it, and what did you learn?"

- "Describe a victory you experienced in maintaining your commitment to purity. How did you feel, and how did it impact your faith?"

3. **Questions and Doubts:**

- "What questions or doubts do you have about God's design for sexuality? How can you seek answers through prayer and scripture?"

- "Is there a particular aspect of your faith that you find challenging? Write about it and pray for clarity and strength."

4. Gratitude and Prayer:

- "List three things you are grateful for today. How do these blessings reflect God's love and care for you?"

- "Write a prayer asking God for guidance and strength in your journey toward sexual purity."

5. Future Goals and Aspirations:

- "What are your goals for your relationships and personal growth? How can you align these goals with God's plan for your life?"

- "Describe the person you want to become in the next five years. How can your faith and commitment to purity help you achieve this?"

Recommended Books and Online Resources

Reading books and exploring online resources can provide additional insights and support as you navigate questions about sexuality, relationships, and faith. Here are some recommended resources to help you grow in your understanding and commitment to God's design for your life.

Recommended Books

1. Every Young Man's Battle" by Stephen Arterburn and Fred Stoeker:
    - Focuses on the challenges young men face regarding sexual purity

and offers practical advice for overcoming temptation.

2. Every Young Woman's Battle" by Shannon Ethridge and Stephen Arterburn:

- Addresses the unique struggles young women encounter and provides guidance for maintaining sexual integrity.

3. **Sex Matters" by Jonathan McKee:**

- Explores the biblical perspective on sex and relationships, offering practical tips for living out God's plan for sexuality.

4. Boundaries in Dating" by Dr. Henry Cloud and Dr. John Townsend:

    - Helps you understand the importance of setting boundaries in relationships to maintain purity and respect.

5. True Love Dates" by Debra Fileta:

    - Provides a roadmap for healthy, God-centered dating relationships and emphasizes the importance of emotional and spiritual connection.

Online Resources

i. **Focus on the Family:**

    - Offers a wealth of articles, podcasts, and videos on topics related to sexuality, relationships, and faith.

ii. **Pure Life Ministries:**

- Provides resources and support for overcoming sexual temptation and living a life of purity.

iii. **The Rebelution:**

- A blog and community focused on encouraging young people to live countercultural lives that honor God.

iv. **Covenant Eyes:**

- Offers accountability software and resources to help you stay pure online.

v. Desiring God:

- Features articles and sermons on various topics, including sexuality and relationships, from a biblical perspective.

Apps for Accountability and Filtering Content

In today's digital age, it's important to use technology wisely. There are several apps designed to help you stay accountable and filter inappropriate content, ensuring that your online activities align with your commitment to purity.

Recommended Apps

1) Covenant Eyes:

- Provides internet accountability and filtering services. It monitors your online activities and sends reports to your accountability partner.

2) Accountable2You:

- Tracks your device usage and sends detailed reports to your chosen accountability partners. It also offers real-time alerts for potentially inappropriate content.

3) Ever Accountable:

- Similar to Covenant Eyes, it monitors your online activities and provides accountability reports to your partners.

4) Net Nanny:

- A comprehensive internet filter that blocks inappropriate content and allows parents to monitor and manage their children's online activities.

5) Bark:

- Monitors text messages, emails, and social media for signs of inappropriate content, cyberbullying, and other potential risks. It provides alerts to parents and accountability partners.

How to Use These Apps Effectively

<u>i.</u> **Choose a Trusted Accountability Partner:** Select someone you trust and who shares your commitment to purity. This could be a parent, mentor, or close friend.

<u>ii.</u> **Be Honest and Open:** Transparency is key. Share your struggles and victories with your accountability partner regularly.

<u>iii.</u> **Set Up Alerts and Reports:** Configure the app to send regular reports and real-time alerts to your accountability partner.

<u>iv.</u> **Use Filters and Blockers:** Take advantage of the app's filtering features to block inappropriate content and create a safe online environment.

<u>v.</u> **Stay Committed:** Consistently use the app and remain committed to your goals of maintaining purity and honoring God with your online activities.

CONCLUSION

Well, dear friends, we've taken quite an adventurous trek together through the sacred terrain of sexuality - this core part of our identity that so few find words to describe with depth and resonance. From discovering the very fingerprints of our Creators in the intricate details of our bodies, to wrestling with modern cultural forces that seek to distort intimacy, to exploring the heights and valleys of romantic relationships, not a single aspect of this human experience has gone unturned.

If you're anything like me, you're likely walking away from these pages with an utterly transformed perspective on what it means to understand and steward sexuality through the lens of the Gospel. A beautiful, at times disruptive truth has been uncovered: Our desires, our bodies, our immense capacity to experience intimacy and vulnerability and passion – it is all a profound gift from a loving Father who longs for us to experience the fullness of His design.

This journey was never about following a formula or ticking off a rigid list of dos and don'ts. Rather, it was an extended meditation on the mysteries and marvels of our sexuality - the ways it draws us nearer to the heart of God through its creative power, its revelatory nature, its ability to bind human hearts together like nothing else in this earthly realm.

Along the way, we didn't shy away from the raw struggles and complexities involved in honoring this divine design. Sexual brokenness, lust, porn's ubiquitous lure, dating's errant pitfalls, the wounds of objectification – we brought every depraved expression of our sexuality into the healing light of truth to be redeemed and restored.

Yet as excruciating as some of those moments may have been to process, the reward is perhaps the most treasured reality any human heart can experience: abundant life in Christ. True purity, freedom, and ever-deepening intimacy with our Creators and those we love. An eternity spent exploring the richness of Divine Beauty and the manifold ways it's expressed across the cosmos.

So where do we go from here?

For some of you, these pages represent a commissioning of sorts - a sacred calling to take this reclaimed vision of sexuality into your spheres of influence with courage and grace. To become the change-makers and advocates our churches and communities so desperately need. To stand uncompromisingly for truth amidst a culture desperately craving authenticity. To carry forth the blazing torch of passion and joy and life-giving theology revealed in these pages.

To my brothers who have traveled this journey with me, know this: you are set apart as modern-day warriors, holy bellwethers of masculinity reimagined through the prism of Christ's perfection. You are entrusted with the sacred duty of protecting intimacy from toxic distortions, by honoring women as co-heirs in the Kingdom, and by manifesting the strength and tenderness of our Savior in your romantic pursuit of His daughters.

And to my sisters - my queens, my fearless co-heirs in this revolutionary work, you are the precious bearers of divine mystery and beauty unparalleled in all creation. Created in the image of Heavenly Royalty, every nuance of your femininity is meant to serve as a mirror, a signpost drawing the wandering human gaze toward the loveliness of your Creator. May you walk in the bold power of this calling, leaving trails of exodus from our cultural wasteland, liberating others into the Eden of intimacy with God and one another.

For others of you, these pages were likely a salve and sanctuary from the trauma and toxic cycles plaguing your journey with sexuality. You are seen, you are loved, and you are already being redeemed by the work of Christ within your story. Where shame has left you shattered, may His perfect love drive out every lie that has bound you. Where deep wounds have manifested, may you encounter the intimate embrace and healing caress of the Wonderful Counselor Himself.

And for those who find yourself in neither of those camps - those who perhaps picked up this work out of sheer curiosity or a nagging sense that something more transcendent must exist beyond the status quo - may the revelations contained here serve as a wake-up call to the deepest yearnings of your spirit. An invitation not just into freedom, but into the full force of intimacy with your Makers, into co-laboring with them to cultivate gardens of beauty wherever your feet shall roam.

Regardless of where we've each arrived at the closing of this journey, one core reality remains: We are forever transformed by having beheld the blazing holiness of sex and intimacy as our Creators intended. We cannot uncross that sacred threshold into vulnerability, tenderness, playfulness, passion, trust, and awe. Forever, we remain ruined for anything less than this eternal vision of human sexuality – this experience of unshakable, all-consuming intimacy that allows all Divine Pleasures to resound across the vast expanse.

So let us go forth as agents of this intimacy – co-crafters of a transcendent sexuality always drawing ourselves and others into deeper encounters with perfect, all-consuming Love. A daring force radically committed to the ancient dream of at last beholding the Divine with undressed gaze, in the ecstatic fullness for which all of creation groans in expectant longing.

It's been my great honor to explore these mysteries alongside you. May all your nights henceforth blaze with revelations, and all your days intoxicate with inexplicable bliss.

Emmanuel – God is with us. In naked majesty and mystery. Always.

Michelle Dane-Smith

APPENDIX

A. Bible Study Guide: Key Verses on Sexuality

Studying the Bible helps us understand God's design for sexuality and relationships. Here are key verses to guide your study:

6. Genesis 1:27-28

"So, God created mankind in his own image, in the image of God he created them; male and female he created them. God blessed them and said to them, 'Be fruitful and increase in number; fill the earth and subdue it.'"

Discussion: Discuss what it means to be created in God's image and how this impacts our understanding of sexuality and gender.

7. **Genesis 2:24**

   "That is why a man leaves his father and mother and is united to his wife, and they become one flesh."

   Discussion: Talk about the significance of marriage and the concept of becoming one flesh.

8. **1 Corinthians 6:18-20**

   "Flee from sexual immorality. All other sins a person commits are outside the body, but whoever sins sexually, sins against their own body. Do you not know that your bodies are temples of the Holy Spirit, who is in you, whom you have received from God? You are not your own; you were bought at a price. Therefore, honor God with your bodies."

Discussion: Explore what it means to honor God with our bodies and why sexual purity is important.

9. **Hebrews 13:4**

   "Marriage should be honored by all, and the marriage bed kept pure, for God will judge the adulterer and all the sexually immoral."

   Discussion: Reflect on the importance of purity within marriage and God's view on sexual immorality.

10. **Psalm 139:13-14**

    "For you created my inmost being; you knit me together in my mother's womb. I praise you because I am fearfully and wonderfully made; your works are wonderful; I know that full well."

Discussion: Discuss how knowing we are fearfully and wonderfully made influences our self-worth and relationships.

11. Song of Solomon 8:4

"Daughters of Jerusalem, I charge you: Do not arouse or awaken love until it so desires."

Discussion: Talk about the wisdom of waiting for the right time for love and sexual intimacy.

12. Ephesians 5:3

"But among you there must not be even a hint of sexual immorality, or of any kind of impurity, or of greed, because these are improper for God's holy people."

Discussion: Explore what it means to live a life free from sexual immorality and impurity.

B. Conversation Starters for Parents and Teens

Open and honest communication between parents and teens is essential for navigating the complexities of sexuality. Here are some conversation starters to help facilitate meaningful discussions:

i. Understanding Changes

- **Parent:** "What changes have you noticed in your body or emotions recently?"
- **Teen:** Share any physical or emotional changes you've been experiencing.

ii. Setting Boundaries

- **Parent:** "Let's talk about why setting boundaries in relationships is important. What boundaries do you think are necessary?"

- **Teen:** Discuss your thoughts on boundaries and why they matter.

iii. Peer Pressure

- **Parent:** "How do you handle peer pressure when it comes to dating and relationships?"

- **Teen:** Share your experiences with peer pressure and how you respond to it.

iv. Media Influence

- **Parent:** "How do you feel media and social media influence our views on sex and relationships?"

- **Teen:** Talk about specific examples from media and how they affect your perceptions.

v. God's Design for Sex

- **Parent:** "What do you think about God's design for sex as described in the Bible?"

- **Teen:** Reflect on your understanding of God's design for sex and how it shapes your views.

vi. Emotional Health

- **Parent:** "How do you feel about your emotional health in relation to your friendships and relationships?"

- **Teen:** Share how your relationships impact your emotional well-being.

vii. Seeking Guidance

- **Parent:** "Who do you feel comfortable talking to about questions or concerns regarding sex and relationships?"

- **Teen:** Identify trusted adults or mentors you can turn to for advice.

C. Self-Care Checklist for Emotional and Physical Health

Taking care of your emotional and physical health is crucial during your journey. Here's a checklist to help you maintain balance and well-being:

1. Emotional Health

- **Daily Journaling:** Write down your thoughts, feelings, and experiences.

- **Prayer and Meditation:** Spend time in prayer and meditation to center your mind and spirit.

- **Talk to Someone:** Regularly communicate with a trusted friend, mentor, or counselor.

- **Engage in Hobbies:** Participate in activities that bring you joy and relaxation.

- **Mindfulness Practices:** Practice mindfulness exercises like deep breathing or yoga.

2. Physical Health

- **Balanced Diet:** Eat a variety of healthy foods to fuel your body.

- **Regular Exercise:** Engage in physical activities you enjoy, like sports, dancing, or walking.

- **Adequate Sleep:** Aim for 8-10 hours of sleep each night.

- **Hygiene Practices:** Maintain good hygiene, including regular bathing, dental care, and grooming.

- Visit your doctor for regular health check-ups and any concerns.

3. Mental Health

- **Positive Affirmations:** Speak positive affirmations to yourself daily.

- **Limit Screen Time:** Manage your screen time to avoid digital overload.

- **Creative Outlets:** Engage in creative activities like drawing, writing, or playing an instrument.

- **Stress Management:** Identify stressors and find healthy ways to manage them, such as through exercise or hobbies.

- **Seek Professional Help:** Don't hesitate to seek professional help if you're feeling overwhelmed or anxious.

4. Spiritual Health

- **Bible Study:** Spend time reading and studying the Bible.

- **Church Involvement:** Participate in church activities and youth groups.

- **Serve Others:** Find opportunities to serve others in your community.

- **Worship:** Spend time in worship through music, prayer, or other forms of expression.

- **Spiritual Mentorship:** Seek guidance from spiritual mentors or leaders in your church.